Building a Christ-Centered Home

A Thomas Nelson Study Series
Based on *The Journey*
by
BILLY GRAHAM

THOMAS NELSON
Since 1798

NASHVILLE   DALLAS   MEXICO CITY   RIO DE JANEIRO   BEIJING

Published in Nashville, Tennessee. Thomas Nelson is a trademark of Thomas Nelson, Inc.

Thomas Nelson, Inc., titles may be purchased in bulk for educational, business, fund-raising, or sales promotional use. For information, please e-mail SpecialMarkets@ThomasNelson.com.

Unless otherwise noted, all Scripture quotations are taken from *The Holy Bible*, NEW INTERNATIONAL VERSION®. NIV®. Copyright © 1973, 1978, 1984 by International Bible Society. Used by permission of Zondervan. All rights reserved.

Building a Christ-Centered Home: A Thomas Nelson Study Series Based on The Journey *by Billy Graham*

ISBN-13: 978-1-4185-1768-7
ISBN-10: 1-4185-1768-2

Printed in the United States of America
07 08 09 10 11 RRD 5 4 3 2 1

Building a
Christ-Centered
Home

The Journey Study Series

Searching for Hope
Living as a Christian
Leaving a Legacy
Dealing with Doubt
Confronting the Enemies Within
Embracing the Good News
Building a Christ-Centered Home
Learning to Pray
The Facilitator's Guide

Contents

1. One Day at a Time / 1

2. Forks in the Road / 21

3. For Better or for Worse / 41

4. Being a Family / 61

5. Broken Dreams / 79

6. Preventive Medicine / 97

Notes / 119

1

One Day at a Time

T O GET THE MOST FROM THIS STUDY GUIDE, READ
pages 227–236 of *The Journey.*

---

*Many things can disrupt our journey through life if
we aren't careful. Life is full of daily challenges and
minor annoyances. And unless we take measure to
prevent it, they will smother our faith.*

BILLY GRAHAM
The Journey

THINK ABOUT IT

*I determined never to stop until I had come to the end
and achieved my purpose.*

—DAVID LIVINGSTONE[1]

*Let us throw off everything that hinders and the sin that so
easily entangles, and let us run with perseverance the race
marked out for us.*

—HEBREWS 12:1

A college student once quipped that he just wanted to get through one day without having a major life event take place. Maybe you can echo his sentiments. Life seems to come at us faster than we like. From nagging aches and pains to major catastrophes, none of us is immune to the small and large problems of life.

Occasionally, someone will get the idea that a believer's life will be free of problems. That's not true. Believers do have the advantage of God's presence when dealing with problems, but the problems persist. Some even argue that Satan's attacks on believers may cause them to experience more problems than non-believers.

REWIND

Think back over the past twenty-four hours and list the problems you have encountered.

_____

_____

_____

What has been the overall spiritual effect of these problems?

_____ **I have been made spiritually stronger.**

_____ **I have been made spiritually weaker.**

_____ **The problems had no spiritual effect.**

_____ **I haven't thought about it.**

One of the challenges of living in a family is that the issues demanding our attention seem to multiply. Not only do we get to handle the problems we face, but we also face the problems of our family members. If we aren't careful, the pressures of life will suffocate our faith and we'll find ourselves wondering what happened.

JOURNEY THROUGH GOD'S WORD

What does the Bible mean when it refers to "worldliness"? It has to do with the concept of the world and its effect on our spiritual lives. The "world" is used to describe the spirit of evil that permeates the culture in which we live. In the writings of John, the world is painted in a particularly negative light.

People who are governed by the world lack the ability to understand the significance of the cross and the death of Jesus Christ as the atonement for sin. The world is described as being dark and without hope. To counter the darkness, Jesus Christ brought light to keep us from being tripped up in the darkness.

So, we understand what the world is, but what is worldliness? Worldliness is the worship of the things of the world. In Colossians 3:5, Paul instructed us to put to death the worldliness in our lives. Many things of the world are not inherently evil or bad. What makes them bad is their use or abuse. Whenever anything in the world is used for purposes other than those designed by God, it is wrong.

Peter described the world as being corrupt or lacking the ability to be good. This is a reference to the spiritual effects of the world—it cannot point you to God without the intervention of the Holy Spirit (2 Peter 1:4). James said that anyone who is in a relationship with the world is committing spiritual adultery (James 4:4). John discouraged followers of Christ from loving the world and the things in it (1 John 2:15).

Spiritual rebirth (or salvation) brings about the death of a person to the world and awakens the person to spiritual life (Galatians 6:14). Jesus warned that pursuit of the world and its pleasures is dangerous (Matthew 16:26).[2]

What does it mean? It means that the pressure to seek the world and its pleasures is a natural desire. The only defense we have against the desire is the presence of the Holy Spirit in our lives. Even then, the pressures of the world can become more of a focus than our spiritual obligations, and the Spirit can be choked out in our lives. It's not that the Spirit leaves us, we just allow other things to influence our actions more than we allow God to influence us. This is why so many believers are spiritually lethargic and frustrated.

As we walk through the halls of our churches, we encounter people just like us—they have problems and issues they are facing. Only as we work together to allow God to live through us can we overcome the problems and stay focused on God's desires for us.

RETHINK

Describe a time when your faith in God went cold.

_____

_____

_____

_____

What caused the situation described above?

_____

_____

_____

Biblical characters weren't exempt from the pressures of worldliness. The story of Demas is a good example of what happens
when someone falls in love with the things of the world. Demas
was one of Paul's companions and had been an integral part of
the spread of the gospel of Jesus Christ (Colossians 4:14;
Philemon 1:24). When Paul was imprisoned, Demas stayed close
by. Demas, however, got distracted and began to see the world
as more attractive than his faith relationship.

Read 2 Timothy 4:10. What was the cause of Demas' downfall?

_____

_____

_____

If you search the Scripture, you will never find another mention of Demas. In spite of the potential he had and the work he did, he disappears—just like many people who at one time expressed faith in Jesus Christ but never lived up to their potential in life or in faith.

What is something you bought but never used as you intended?

_____

_____

_____

_____

_____

One of the most popular categories of items in a garage sale is exercise equipment. With good intentions, people purchase everything from treadmills to weight machines and pledge to get in shape. But it was easier to purchase the equipment than to use it so it eventually is sold for a fraction of its original cost. Good intentions don't make one exercise physically or spiritually.

When you first accepted Jesus Christ as Lord, what were your spiritual intentions?

_____

_____

_____

Have you kept those intentions alive? Why or why not?

_____

_____

_____

REFLECT

On average, how many hours do you spend each day doing the following?

_____ Sleep

_____ Work (including commuting)

_____ Housework (including yard work)

_____ Taking care of the needs of your children

_____ Preparing meals, eating, and cleaning up

_____ Hobbies

_____ Using the computer (other than work)

_____ Entertainment (television, music, movies)

_____ Shopping

_____ Doing schoolwork

_____ Going to church

_____ Reading the Bible and praying

_____ Attending social events and meetings

_____ Other: _____

_____ TOTAL

Most people today are either too busy—or not busy enough. Either our schedules are so hectic we can't get everything done, or else we are bored and restless, constantly looking for something to amuse us. The Bible, however, tells us that both extremes are wrong.

BILLY GRAHAM
The Journey

If you're like most people, you are busy. It's not surprising that your total might have exceeded twenty-four hours because you often do several things on the list at the same time. We call it multitasking. That's a more positive term than "too busy"!

The pressures of time management are almost universal. In spite of predictions, we don't seem to have more free time than did our parents and grandparents. When the pressure is on, it's easy to eliminate one or more things from the list. One of the first things to go for many people is their time with God.

If time doesn't push God away, the pressure of the crowd will. Pressure at work and from friends can cause a believer to keep his or her faith a secret. It can become so much of a secret that even the believer forgets about it.

If time and the crowd don't affect your faith, sin will. Without a steady prayer life, sin goes unconfessed. Like we have mentioned several times, unconfessed sin puts a barrier between us and God. We feel defeated because our sinful nature is in control and we give up on our relationship with God.

If time, the crowd, and sin aren't enough, our spiritual lives often degenerate because we abandon our commitment to spiritual growth.

Read 2 Peter 3:18. What is the command in this verse?

_____

_____

_____

If we are going to be effective in our spiritual lives, we must begin to use our time wisely. Wasted time can never be recaptured. Here are some biblical principles for time management.

1. **See each day as a gift from God.**
   This is one of the easiest things to overlook. God didn't have to give you today; He could have called you home before your sleep was done. The very fact that you are breathing is evidence that God loves you.

Read Psalm 31:15. What was the attitude of the psalmist toward the day?

_____

_____

_____

_____

2. **Commit your time to God.**
   God left you here today for a reason. The abundant life is only possible as you live out God's purposes. When you begin to live for yourself, you discover frustration and disappointment. Your only option is to live for God.

Read Psalm 90:12. What is the end result of giving God your time?

_____

_____

_____

How have you seen God's wisdom at work in your life?

_____

_____

_____

3. **Set aside time for God and others.**

    Are you too busy for God? Sometimes it seems that way, doesn't it? When we get too busy, we begin to ignore spending time with God and meeting the needs of others. We get so focused on the pressures we face that we exclude from consideration anyone or anything that doesn't have something to do with our lives.

Describe the last time you spent meeting the needs of a friend.

_____

_____

_____

_____

> *We all need rest and recreation; God made us this way. If Jesus required times of rest, don't we also? Someone who is chronically exhausted from lack of sleep or improper eating is much more susceptible to Satan's attacks.*
>
> BILLY GRAHAM
> *The Journey*

4. **Take time for your own needs.**

   We need rest and relaxation; God built that need into our design and provided the Sabbath and sleep for those purposes. Never feel guilty about taking time off. Make rest as important and necessary as work.

Read Mark 6:31. Describe the place where you can be quiet and get some rest.

_____

_____

_____

_____

What about your vocation? How does your faith connect to your work inside or outside your home? Some people see no connection, but the Bible teaches us something different.

In the Bible, work is commanded. Before the Fall, Adam was charged with tending the Garden of Eden. After the Fall, the call to work continued, but the ground was hardened and overgrown, and work made more difficult. The bottom line is that God wants to work through your job to accomplish His purposes. How can that happen?

1. _View your work as a God-given responsibility._
   God put you in your job so that He can work through your life.

Read Ecclesiastes 2:24. How satisfying is your work? Explain your response.

_____

_____

_____

_____

2. *Be faithful in your work.*

Many employers complain about the lack of motivation of their employees. As Christians, we are called to exhibit godliness in all that we do—including work. According to Mark 6:3, Jesus worked and did not sin!

Read Colossians 3:22. What should your attitude be toward your work?

_____

_____

_____

Read Colossians 4:1. If you are an employer, what should your attitude be toward your employees?

_____

_____

_____

_____

3. *Work with integrity.*
    We live in a time when integrity is becoming more and more rare in the workplace. But because of our relationship with God, we don't have the option of being anything other than people of integrity.

Read Ephesians 5:8–11. How does this passage apply to your work?

_____

_____

_____

_____

REACT

Only as you submit your daily life to God can you find real joy in this world. Left unattended, your faith will be taken over by the cares of the world.

In what areas of life are you most likely to encounter problems?

_____

_____

_____

Pray, asking God to give you wisdom so that you can deal with the issues of life without sacrificing your faith. As you read the Bible, pray, and interact with other believers, you will be strengthened in your walk and better prepared to handle life's problems, no matter how large or how small.

> *Don't let life's routines smother your faith, but submit your whole self (including your time and your work) to Christ's authority every day.*
>
> BILLY GRAHAM
> *The Journey*

What are three truths you learned in this study, and how will you apply each truth to your daily life?

1. _____

_____

_____

_____

2. _____

_____

_____

_____

3. _____

_____

_____

_____

2

Forks
in the
Road

T O GET THE MOST FROM THIS STUDY GUIDE, READ pages 237–246 of *The Journey*.

We can't change the past, but we can change the future. One of the most important skills we can ever develop in life is the ability to make wise choices.

BILLY GRAHAM
The Journey

THINK ABOUT IT

We must, like Paul, forget everything that is behind us, refusing to allow the dead hand of the past to be laid upon our present or future, and turn a deaf ear to the satanic suggestion that the past, with its failures . . . is only the prophecy of the future.

—J. GREGORY MANTLE[1]

I will instruct you and teach you in the way you should go;
I will counsel you and watch over you.

—PSALM 32:8

We all wish we could go back and undo some of the mistakes we have made. Some people actually try but have little success. Some people believe they are destined to repeat the past, while others show determination to distance themselves from the past.

One thing we know—we all make mistakes and pay the price for those mistakes. Like the Bible says, we do reap what we sow (Galatians 6:7). Some people just don't seem to be able to connect their actions to the consequences. They live with a victim mentality that suggests they are just innocent victims of a big bad world. But often we are victims of our own bad decisions and choices. When we come to a fork in the road, we need to be better equipped to follow God's leadership and make wise decisions.

REWIND

What is God's will for your life?

_____

_____

_____

How are you living out that will in your daily life?

_____

_____

_____

Contrary to what we sometimes think, God knows everything we think before we think it and everything we do before we do it. Our rebellion is no surprise to Him. Sometimes, the only people surprised by our thoughts and actions are us.

God, however, has a will or a plan for your life. He gives you the choice of living according to His plan or not living according to His plan. God's will is a function of His love for us. He wants what's best and has a path that leads to the best for us. Our journey through life leads us through a series of intersections and forks in the road where we must discern God's voice and hear His call. Otherwise, we end up too far down the path of disobedience.

JOURNEY THROUGH GOD'S WORD

The will of God is His plan and purpose for His people. There are two facts we must keep straight—God does what

---

He pleases, and He desires that we do whatever pleases Him. We often get it backwards—we believe that we can do whatever we please and that God is obligated to please us. This is a misinterpretation of Scripture.

As believers mature, they are better able to do God's will consistently. An inconsistent commitment to doing God's will is a sign of spiritual immaturity (Colossians 4:12). We never have to wonder if God's will is good; it always is the best thing for us, even if the world tells us something different. God's will is perfect, and doing God's will sustains us.

Doing the will of God, however, can lead to suffering and persecution (James 1:2–4). Even though we encounter difficulties, doing God's will still produces the best possible life.

Christians are to pursue God's will for their lives (Psalm 143:10) and to seek God's will through prayer (Colossians 1:9) and the study of God's Word (Psalm 119:105).

Some people want to choose a course of action and convince God that it is the best for them. God, however, isn't into negotiating His will for our lives. Doing anything less than being obedient to God's will is a sin, and we live with the consequences of our disobedience.

If God didn't love us, He wouldn't be concerned about our obedience to His will. Yet God does love us. He loves us so much that He was willing to sacrifice His Son, Jesus Christ, so that we might have eternal life. Our lives should be lived in gratitude for all that God has done to establish our relationship with Him.

RETHINK

Does God really care about the decisions we make? The Bible's answer is clear: God knows all about us, and He knows what is best for us. He sees the dangers we face, and He also knows the joys we could experience. But God not only knows what is best for us, He also wants what is best for us. The reason is simple: He loves us.

BILLY GRAHAM
The Journey

What aspects of life are not included in God's will?

_____ Employment

_____ Family

_____ Spiritual growth

_____ Social activities

_____ Hobbies

_____ Relationships

_____ Ambitions

_____ Education

_____ Entertainment

_____ Other: _____

How often do you ask, "Is this God's will for me?"

_____ Hourly

_____ Daily

_____ Weekly

_____ Monthly

_____ Never

God's will has two dimensions—His general will and His individual will. God's general will is His will for all people. It has to do with morality and ethics. Throughout Scripture, we see evidence of God's giving His general will to His people. These are principles by which to live.

Where can you find God's general will?

_____ Legal documents

_____ The Bible

_____ The newspaper

_____ Television

_____ The latest poll

Read 2 Timothy 3:16. God gave us the Bible for what purposes?

_____

_____

_____

_____

The Bible contains specific guidelines—it tells us when something is right or wrong. When the Bible says something is wrong, it is wrong for all people at all times.

What are the specific guidelines in the following passages?

Romans 13:7

_____

_____

_____

_____

1 Corinthians 6:18

_____

_____

_____

_____

The Bible also contains principles that can be applied to any situation. Jesus taught His followers to love all people. This is a principle that should govern every area of life.

Read Luke 10:27. What is the principle contained in this verse?

_____

_____

_____

_____

The second dimension of God's will is the individual will. God's personal will differs from person to person. Because God knows us, He has a plan that will result in His best for us.

Read Jeremiah 29:11. What is the general nature of God's personal will for you?

_____

_____

_____

REFLECT

> *We claim we want God's will—but then we rush off in all directions, frantically trying to decide what to do without ever pausing to ask God to guide us. Or sometimes we assume we already know which way is best—although God may have other plans for us. Don't let this happen to you, but commit every decision to Him.*
>
> BILLY GRAHAM
> *The Journey*

How can we discover God's will for our lives? Some people just try several things hoping to land on the right one. Others seek advice from books hoping to learn a trick from someone else. There are six things you can do to discover God's will.

1. **Commit your decision to God.**
   Seek God's advice regarding His will for you. It is not God's plan to keep His will hidden from you. Ask God to reveal to you anything that might inter-fere with your ability to see and do His will. Then, repent and ask God to make you open and obedient to His will.

Read Psalm 86:11. Who is the teacher?

_____

Who is the learner?

_____

Is this a reality in your life? Why or why not?

_____

_____

_____

2. Search the Scriptures.

The Bible gives us direction regarding the decisions we are making. We must understand that God will never tell us to do something that is contradictory to Scripture. We sometimes decide what we want to do and then force the Scripture to go along with us. We have to make sure that we are handling the Scripture in a way that is in line with its real meaning. Otherwise, we will make Scripture speak untruths, and we will make bad decisions.

Think about your most recent major decision. What does Scripture say (directly or in principle) about the situation you were facing?

_____

_____

_____

_____

_____

_____

3. **Understand your circumstances.**

   Sometimes God uses our circumstances to guide us in the way we should go. When God wants us to do something, He may prepare the way for us to understand it through our circumstances. God also can use our circumstances to prevent us from doing something. You might have experienced a situation that was tough to handle yet, in the end, you realized it was God's way of getting you on the path He had for you.

Describe a time when you discovered God's will with the help of the circumstances you faced.

_____

_____

_____

4. **Seek godly advice.**

   People often make the mistake of seeking spiritual advice from the least likely sources. Would you seek advice on fixing your car's transmission from someone who doesn't know anything about cars? Why, then, would you seek spiritual advice from someone who doesn't know anything about God and His Word?

Read Proverbs 15:22. From whom should you be seeking advice?

_____

_____

_____

Do you have a group of spiritual advisors you can depend on to help guide your thinking? The Bible is correct in its assertion that there is wisdom in surrounding ourselves with people who love God.

It is equally dangerous to submit to the influence of people who do not know Jesus Christ as Lord and Savior. Their advice, though well-intended, isn't grounded in Scripture and, therefore, it may not represent truth.

5. **Trust the guidance of the Holy Spirit.**

   Once we get to know God, we are more aware of the promptings of the Holy Spirit. God speaks to us through inner convictions and peace. We can't always equate God's Spirit with a feeling, however. We also must be aware that the Holy Spirit will not guide us into any action that is prohibited in Scripture.

Read Isaiah 30:21. Describe a time when you have had a situation like the one described in this verse.

_____

_____

_____

_____

Read John 16:13. How can you tell the difference between your desires and the prompting of the Holy Spirit?

_____

_____

_____

_____

6. **Trust God for the outcome.**

Many times, we pray and then act without having a clear understanding as to what we are supposed to do. We grow impatient and expect God to act on our schedule. In reality, we might be stepping out of God's will and creating a situation that is far removed from His plan for our lives. On the other hand, sometimes God wants us to step out in faith, trusting that He is with us and He is guiding us.

If a decision is of God, He will remain in it. God doesn't stand at the top of the mountain, give us a push, and then hope for the best. God is an integral part of all that we do. Therefore, we must begin to take one step at a time while making sure that God is with us for the journey.

Read Proverbs 3:5–6. What are the instructions in this passage?

_____

_____

_____

_____

What is the end result in this passage?

_____

_____

_____

_____

REACT

You might be questioning God's will for your life right now. Maybe this has been a long process for you. It could be that God is telling you to do something that you aren't willing to do. It could be that you are listening to the wrong advice. It also could be that you are not tuned in to God at all.

What is keeping you from hearing God's will for your life?

_____

_____

_____

Seeking God's will is just the first step in the process. We must discover God's will and then do it. Suppose it was your birthday and you received a gift but refused to open it. What value is that gift to you? The same holds true for discovering God's will. Once you find God's will, you must be willing to act on it, depending on Him to help you.

What is the end result of knowing and doing God's will? Personal peace and a sense of purpose are two things that are immediate results. You will never have more joy in life than you will when you are doing what God designed you to do. It's a matter of choice. What will you do?

> *Remember God loves you, and He wants you to do His will. Seek it . . . discover it . . . and then do it. His way is always best.*
>
> BILLY GRAHAM
> *The Journey*

What are three truths you learned in this study, and how will you apply each truth to your daily life?

1. _____

_____

_____

2. _____

_____

_____

3. _____

_____

_____

3

For Better or for Worse

T O GET THE MOST FROM THIS STUDY GUIDE, READ pages 247–251 of *The Journey*.

> *The most important truth we need to know about marriage is that God gave it to us. Marriage is God's invention, not ours!*
>
> BILLY GRAHAM
> *The Journey*

THINK ABOUT IT

A good marriage is like an incredible retirement fund. You put everything you have into it during your productive life, and over the years it turns from silver to gold to platinum.
—WILLARD SCOTT[1]

For this reason a man will leave his father and mother and be united to his wife, and they will become one flesh.
—GENESIS 2:24

There is a lot of controversy about marriage and what it really is. Some want to redefine it. Others want to avoid it. Some seem to have no opinion of it at all. Some people have a marriage that seems more like a business partnership, while others have a marriage that resembles the closest friendship.

Whether you are married or not, you have an opinion about marriage. The real question is, however, not what you think about marriage but what God thinks about it. As we have discovered already, what God said in Scripture isn't up for debate or update; it is truth yesterday, today, and forever.

REWIND

What is your definition of marriage?

_____

_____

_____

What are the roles of the husband and wife in marriage?

_____

_____

_____

Marriage is more than just enjoying the company of another person. It is a God-ordained union between a man and a woman. When we revisit the story of the first man and woman, we discover that God had a specific purpose for uniting them.

Read Genesis 2:18. What was God's intention when the woman was created?

_____

_____

_____

Read Genesis 2:21–23. What was different about the creation of woman?

_____

_____

_____

Society wants to redefine the union God created. Marriage is under attack because a society is only as strong as its interpersonal relationships. If Satan can succeed in destroying the institution of marriage, then he can directly attack God's plan for His people. Whether it is socially popular or not, the biblical truths about marriage still remain true. We do not have the right to take over something God established and define it in ways that suit our own desires.

JOURNEY THROUGH GOD'S WORD

In the Bible, *marriage* is defined as a sacred union between one man and one woman, formed before God with an oath of lifelong love and loyalty. The first marriage between Adam and Eve included an instruction that was repeated by Jesus in Matthew 19:4–6. In marriage, the husband and wife become one flesh, signifying the completeness of the bond they established. Because marriage is a covenant relationship established before God, any violation of the covenant is grounds for God's judgment.

The primary purpose of marriage is the same as man's primary purpose—to glorify God and to enjoy our relationship with Him. There is a correlation between the marriage relationship and Jesus' relationship to the church (Ephesians 5:21–33).

Marriage also provides the system in which the human race is continued and expanded. In Scripture, childbearing is a normal part of the marriage relationship.

The term *helper* used to describe the role of the woman in the creation narrative is not a derogatory term. The same word is used to describe God in Genesis 49:25, Exodus 18:4, Psalm 10:12, and other places. Within the marriage relationship the physical, psychological, mental, emotional, and spiritual health of individuals is nurtured.

The marriage relationship is the ultimate example of love. In 1 Corinthians 13:1–7, we see the characteristics of a healthy marriage—patience, humility, joy, truth, peace, affirmation, and hope.[2]

In its biblical ideal, marriage is the greatest earthly example of godly love. The family is the venue in which the knowledge of God is communicated most effectively.

Your concept of marriage might be affected by the home in which you were raised and your personal experience. But because God sets the standard, there always is room for improvement. Let's take a closer look at the marriage relationship as defined by God.

RETHINK

Describe the best example of a "perfect" marriage you've ever seen.

_____

_____

_____

Is it possible for you to have a marriage like that? Why or why not?

_____

_____

_____

What makes marriage special? Basically, it is special because God gave it to us. God, not society, invented marriage. Before sin entered the world, marriage was already in place. Throughout the creation story, we hear God declare His creation to be good or very good. However, He did find one thing that was determined to not be good.

Read Genesis 2:18. What did God say was not good?

_____

_____

_____

_____

Before Eve was created, Adam had a perfect relationship with God. Yet God still declared that man's solitude was not good. He created the woman because the man needed a companion on the earth. Thus, the first family was established.

Read Genesis 2:24. To what extent is this statement true about your marriage or your concept of marriage?

_____ This isn't a real picture of marriage.

_____ This is a nice idea but not reachable.

_____ This is the goal, but it's not working for me.

_____ This is reality for me in my home.

REFLECT

Why did God give us marriage? That might not be a good question to ask your spouse, but it's a great question to ask otherwise! God didn't do anything frivolously; everything has a purpose. Marriage was instituted because God wanted it that way. He defined *marriage* the way it is defined in Scripture because He knew it would be challenged one day. Today, there is so much confusion about marriage, few people can explain what it is and why we have it.

So, why did God give us marriage?

_____

_____

_____

1. **God gave us marriage for our companionship.**
   In the creation story, Adam's search for a companion came up empty. The Bible tells us that "no suitable helper was found" (Genesis 2:20). Because Adam was created in God's image, the ability to love was part of who he was. Not only did he need to express love, but he also needed to be loved.

What is the value to you of a companion?

_____

_____

_____

_____

_____

In addition to having a companion, marriage gives us the opportunity to be good companions. That means putting the needs of our spouse ahead of our needs.

What are some situations in which you are a bit selfish?

_____

_____

_____

_____

How do these situations affect your relationship with your spouse?

_____

_____

_____

2. **God gave us marriage for our mutual help and encouragement.**
   Life is tough, and we all need the encouragement of someone who loves us and cares about us.

Reread Genesis 2:18. The Bible says that Adam needed a companion who was suitable for him. What do you think the word _suitable_ means?

_____

_____

_____

Suitable means several things—"adequate, comparable, similar to"—but it doesn't mean that the woman was subservient.

The woman is described as Adam's helper. They had different roles in the same grand scheme.

Think about your spouse or future spouse. In what ways are you suitable for each other?

_____

_____

_____

_____

> *Adam needed Eve—and Eve needed Adam. I'm always saddened whenever I see a couple drift apart, each living almost as if their spouse didn't exist. It's also tragic to hear a husband or wife tear down their spouse with criticism or verbal abuse. We need each other's constant encouragement and help.*
>
> BILLY GRAHAM
> *The Journey*

Think about the last time you were unexpectedly encouraged by your spouse. Think of something you can do today to encourage your spouse. Prepare a meal, give flowers, go out for dinner . . . just do something to encourage your spouse and to express your love.

3. **God gave us marriage for our mutual happiness and pleasure**.
   After spending his time naming the animals, Adam must have been pleasantly surprised when he encountered another human for the first time.

Read Genesis 2:23. What was Adam's response to Eve's arrival?

_____

_____

_____

_____

God wanted Adam and Eve to bring enjoyment to each other in a number of ways. He wanted them to have a physical relationship that would honor Him. He wanted them to be emotionally attached to and supportive of each other. He wanted them to be intellectually beneficial to each other. He also wanted them to embrace the spiritual life in concert with each other.

In what ways are you fulfilling these purposes in your marriage relationship? If you aren't married, how do you see your future life with your spouse?

_____

_____

_____

_____

God gave Adam and Eve the gift of sex. It probably strikes some of you as odd just to see that word in print. Yet there is nothing wrong with sex the way God intended it. However, our world has perverted what God called good and made it uncomfortable for us to talk about.

The sexual relationship is the ultimate expression of love inside the boundaries of marriage. However, when sex is practiced outside of God's boundaries, the consequences can be tragic.

Reread Genesis 2:24.
The becoming of one flesh is the physical element of the relationship. It is a sign of the couple's unity and a seal of their lasting commitment.

> *God demands sexual purity and faithfulness not because He wants to make us miserable, but because He wants to make us happy. He knows far better than we do that sex outside of marriage always falls short of His perfect plan and can bring heartache and mistrust in its wake.*
>
> BILLY GRAHAM
> *The Journey*

Why can't people just live together without bothering to get married? That question and that practice have become more common in recent years. Even within the church fellowship, there may be situations where people are in relationships that are outside the boundaries of God's plan.

Sex outside of marriage always falls short of God's perfect plan and establishes a relationship outside of God's boundaries. Promiscuity before marriage leads to distrust after marriage.

When an unmarried couple lives together, their relationship lacks trust and commitment. Because there is no commitment, their relationship will never be secure.

Read Proverbs 6:27–29. What is the warning regarding living outside of God's boundaries?

_____

_____

_____

REACT

There are several possible responses to this lesson. First of all, if you are not married, now is the time to make some promises to God that you will not violate. Based on His Word, make a commitment to Him regarding maintaining your sexual purity until marriage. Commit to seeking His guidance in finding the right spouse. And, if God impresses upon you the need to remain celibate, make a commitment to Him that you will not break.

What are some things you can do to better prepare yourself for marriage?

_____

_____

_____

If you are married, sit down with your spouse and make an agreement that you will live within the boundaries that God has established. Commit to making the welfare of the other person your primary relational goal. Make time in your schedule to read and study God's Word together. Become active members in a local congregation, and surround yourself with like-minded believers in Jesus Christ.

In 1 Corinthians 7:39, Paul instructed the Christians in Corinth that who they marry "must belong to the Lord." This indicates that the ideal situation for marriage is for both the bride and groom to be committed followers of Jesus Christ. It is not good for a husband and wife to be "unequally yoked" (see 2 Corinthians 6:14). Marrying a non-believer is a violation of biblical principles. If you are married to a non-believer, begin praying for the salvation of your spouse—but resist the temptation to badger him or her. Let your example of love and a godly character speak louder than your words.

In the space below, list the specific times when you will spend time with your spouse in Bible study and prayer.

_____

_____

_____

Maybe you have been married and for some reason you are no longer married. Don't despair. God is the God of love and forgiveness. Spend time with God asking Him how you can be a better spouse in the future. Allow God to teach you His truths as you work through this situation. Then, whatever happens in the future, commit yourself to honoring God in your family.

A husband and wife need a loving and lasting commitment to each other.

BILLY GRAHAM
The Journey

The real challenge is to be the people God intended us to be. That means being like Christ in our willingness to lay down our lives for someone else. Marriage is not all about you and what you get; it's about honoring God in life as you work together as a team.

What are three truths you learned in this study, and how will you apply each truth to your daily life?

1. _____

_____

_____

_____

2. _____

_____

_____

_____

3. _____

_____

_____

_____

4

Being
a
Family

T O GET THE MOST FROM THIS STUDY GUIDE, READ
pages 251–256 of *The Journey.*

Children need instruction and love if they are to become
responsible, mature adults—and in God's design for the
human race, that need was to be fulfilled within the
security of the family.

BILLY GRAHAM
The Journey

THINK ABOUT IT

In the homes of America are born the children of America,
and from them go out into American life American men
and women. They go out with the stamp of these homes
upon them, and only as these homes are what they should
be, will they be what they should be.

—JOSIAH G. HOLLAND[1]

Sons are a heritage from the LORD, children a reward from him.

—PSALM 127:3

The American home isn't what it used to be. The days of Ward, June, Wally, and Theodore (Beaver) are long gone—if they ever existed at all. Today, the American family is beset with a variety of challenges that earlier generations never knew.

Hardly a week goes by without a news story about the abuse of a child by his or her parents. Elderly citizens are abused by their caregivers. Parents are abused by their children. No element of the family is exempt.

Yet, God has a blueprint for the family. The plan isn't new; it is the same plan He had all along. The problems we see in society today are directly related to the drift away from God's plan and principles. The more we move away from God's plan, the worse the news about the family gets.

REWIND

What is the purpose of the family in your view?

_____

_____

_____

Within the family, what are the greatest challenges?

_____

_____

_____

_____

The family is the ideal setting for human development. Within the family, we learn about love and respect, disappointment and anger, security and protection. In the family, the husband and wife are given the privilege of teaching God's principles and His Word to future generations. The health of our faith is closely connected to the spiritual health of our families.

There is no such thing as a perfect copy machine. If you make a copy of the original document, then copy the copy, the resulting document is a downgrade from the original. If you continue copying successive copies, the resulting copies eventually will become unrecognizable.

That is what has happened in the family. Each generation is more removed from the design than the previous generation. Today's family often bears few similarities to God's original design. Our society bears the marks of families gone bad.

JOURNEY THROUGH GOD'S WORD

It might seem odd, but the Bible does contain references to child abuse. Most of the references involve the mass killing of infants or children. One of the earliest stories happened when the king of Egypt feared the rapidly growing Israelite nation that was living in his land. In order to control the population, he ordered that the male babies in the Israelite camp be killed (Exodus 1:16ff). It was from this mass killing that Moses was spared. In the New Testament, upon hearing that the Savior had been born, Herod ordered the murder of the male babies in Bethlehem (Matthew 2:16). Other references to such actions are found in 2 Kings 3, 16, and 23; Genesis 19; 2 Chronicles 33; and Judges 11.

Whereas many earthly leaders were pictured as being abusive of children, God is pictured as the kind, compassionate Father caring for His child. Ezekiel described Israel as having been a child that was abandoned and eventually nurtured by God (Ezekiel 16:4–14). Psalm 103:13 describes God's compassion on His children. In Luke 11:11–13, Jesus described God as more caring than earthly fathers.

Jesus demonstrated great love and compassion to the children He encountered during His ministry. In Mark 10:13–16, Jesus demonstrated the perfect example of parental love for children.

Paul warned parents not to provoke their children (Ephesians 6:4). This instruction, when analyzed, condemns all forms of abuse and neglect. Additionally, Scripture is consistent in its call for God's people to protect those who are innocent and helpless (Psalm 82:3–4; Jeremiah 22:3).[2] Child abuse isn't always physical; it is abusive for parents to put their personal needs ahead of the needs of their children. Yet, that happens day in and day out in the homes of people who call themselves Christians. Authentic faith is revealed in the way we live our daily lives and in the way we care for those God has entrusted to us.

Your ideas about the family might be closely related to the biblical ideal. If so, it is a testimony to God's sustaining power in your home. However, your family life might be nothing like the biblical example. This is no time to simply excuse your idea as being "just the way you are." It is time to discover and commit to God's design for the family.

RETHINK

When it comes to the spiritual training of the individuals in your family, who has the primary responsibility?

_____ The school system

_____ The government

_____ The church

_____ Parents

Grade yourself on the spiritual leadership you are providing those entrusted to you.

_____ A+

_____ A

_____ B

_____ C

_____ D

_____ F

God gave us marriage to provide an order within which children can be nurtured in their faith. Throughout Scripture, God is described as a loving Father caring for the needs of His children. This image of God is no accident. God provides us with the perfect picture of what it means to care for the needs of someone else.

Think about your life. Rank the following needs according to their priority in your life.

_____ **Children and/or family**

_____ **Employer**

_____ **Home**

_____ **Self**

_____ **Hobbies**

_____ **Church**

_____ **Other:** _____

Your priorities govern your actions. If your family isn't your top priority, then your actions are going to reveal that truth. If you want to check the accuracy of your perceived priorities, just evaluate the way you spend your time. You invest time in those things that matter.

REFLECT

In our imperfect and broken world, our families fall short of God's ideal. There aren't many families these days who have been untouched by one or more of the following—divorce, abuse, neglect, poverty, alcoholism, violence, and death. Because of God's love for us, He has provided a support structure to help us get through life's problems.

Read Psalm 32:10. Who are the people who fulfill this role in your life? How many of them are family members?

_____

_____

_____

Through God's strength, we can become the people and the families God intended us to be. It requires us to continually turn to God for wisdom. The Bible teaches that God gives wisdom to those of His children who ask (James 1:5). In seeking and implementing God's wisdom, our families will better reflect Christ— which is another reason God gave us marriage and our families.

Read Galatians 5:22–23. Which of the following characteristics is your strongest? Mark your answer with an S.

____ Love

____ Joy

____ Peace

____ Patience

____ Kindness

____ Goodness

____ Faithfulness

____ Gentleness

____ Self-control

Which of the characteristics above is your greatest weakness? Mark your answer with a W.

As we interact with each other and with our family members, the world sees a picture of God—good or bad! When we fail to demonstrate godly qualities, we demonstrate ungodly qualities by default. As believers, it is our responsibility to reflect Christ to the world. That reflection begins at home.

But life isn't always the way God intended it to be. In every relationship, there are problems. Today, marriages are an endangered species. Satan knows that the spiritual health of a society depends on the spiritual health of its families. Therefore, if Satan can destroy the marriage, he can negatively affect God's purposes in the world.

> *Even when circumstances are difficult in our families, they must not keep us from striving to do our best. Adam and Eve fell far short of perfection while nurturing their family; one son (Cain) even murdered his brother (Abel). But if they apparently failed with Cain, they still succeeded with Abel. Even when divorce or death or some other problem tears our families apart, we must not give up. God cares about our families even more than we do, and with His help we still can do good things for our children.*
>
> BILLY GRAHAM
> *The Journey*

Satan's first attack on marriage was in the Garden of Eden. Satan instigated a conflict between the man and the woman as they attempted to defend their actions by blaming someone else.

Adam blamed Eve; Eve blamed the serpent. Some things never change.

What is the primary source of strife in your family relationships?

_____ **Money**

_____ **Time**

_____ **Conflict**

_____ **Other:** _____

All of the above can be sources of difficulty. Conflict, however, seems to serve as a broad category for the things that harm our relationships. Some of the conflicts in the family are present before marriage. Many of the problems in a person's family leave deep emotional scars that affect how the individuals respond to each other.

Other problems are created after the marriage takes place. One of the biggest threats to the welfare of the family is money. Because of a lack of agreed-upon priorities, people make purchases that handicap their ability to take care of the basic needs of life. Possessions become a burden, not a blessing. People buy cars, boats, and houses they can't afford in order to impress people they don't know. Meanwhile, inside that house there is great conflict. Money problems in our society are a leading cause of divorce among Christians and non-

Christians. In some situations, money problems lead to other problems—addictions to gambling, alcohol, drugs, and other escape mechanisms.

Read Matthew 6:24. Jesus set two potential masters as mutually exclusive. Take a realistic look at your life and determine which master you are serving. Circle your response below:

God

Money

I'm not sure

Now, circle the appropriate terms in the following statement using your response above: I have chosen to make GOD/ MONEY more important than GOD/MONEY. This decision is GOOD/BAD for my family.

Another problem in our families is spiritual disharmony. The biblical instruction is clear—do not marry unbelievers (2 Corinthians 6:14). Like any other violation of biblical principles, violation of this principle has consequences— unhappiness, mistrust, unfaithfulness, and divorce all are real consequences that people face every day. Some unbelieving spouses eventually do come to faith in God, but the years leading up to that decision can leave permanent scars on the relationship.

REACT

What is the primary cause of marital problems? At the core, the main problem is selfishness.

What are you looking for in your relationships?

_____ **To be made happy**

_____ **To get my way**

_____ **To make others happy**

_____ **To make God happy and, in doing so, make others happy**

Real love isn't a feeling; it's a way of life. We can't establish lasting relationships based on physical attraction or emotions. Successful marriages have at their core a common commitment and a growing faith in Jesus Christ. Marriage isn't a relationship between a man and a woman; it is a relationship between a man, a woman, and God. If God is not a part of the marriage, it is weakened from the start.

Read Matthew 19:6. Who establishes the marriage bond? Who is best qualified to maintain the bond?

_____

_____

_____

In today's world, few people seem to know what true love really is. Is true love accurately pictured on television or in the movies? Do the lives of celebrities reveal true love? What about politicians? Are they governing our land with a godly view of marriage and the family?

True love is described in the words of the apostle Paul. In Philippians 2:4 he wrote, "Each of you should look not only to your own interests, but also to the interests of others."

Based on the verse above, are you living your life with a godly understanding of love? If not, why?

_____

_____

_____

The ultimate example of love is found in the Bible as Jesus Christ abandoned His entitlement in order to become the ultimate sacrifice for my sins and yours. There is no other example of love that comes close to the magnitude of that example.

Read 1 Corinthians 13. Now reread the passage substituting your name for every use of the word *love*. Is this an accurate description of you? If not, what will you do to make it true of you?

_____

_____

_____

There certainly is such a thing as true love—and with God's help we can discover it. He wants to take away our sin and our selfishness and replace them with His love— the kind of love that makes us concerned not just for ourselves but for others.

BILLY GRAHAM
The Journey

What are three truths you learned in this study, and how will you apply each truth to your daily life?

1. _____

_____

_____

_____

2. _____

_____

_____

_____

3. _____

_____

_____

_____

5

Broken
Dreams

T O GET THE MOST FROM THIS STUDY GUIDE, READ
pages 257–260 of *The Journey*.

> *Gardens don't grow by themselves; they need to be tended and cultivated and weeded. The same is true of a marriage.*
>
> BILLY GRAHAM
> *The Journey*

THINK ABOUT IT

Beware of succumbing to failure as inevitable; make it the stepping-stone to success.

—OSWALD CHAMBERS[1]

As for me and my household, we will serve the LORD.

—JOSHUA 24:15

Sheer determination overcomes a lot of obstacles. From climbing mountains to sailing the ocean to marriage, perseverance plays an important role. It is unfortunate that many people enter into a marriage relationship with the idea that their commitment to their spouse is conditional. As long as everything is going good, the marriage seems to work. But let one thing go wrong and they are ready to walk away and start over.

Circus acrobats work with a net because they realize the physical danger associated with a minor slip. For them, the safety net is their insurance policy. In marriage, however, many people see divorce as their safety net and seem to enjoy jumping into it.

Others, however, find themselves signing divorce papers while wondering what happened. This wasn't the plan when their marriages began. This is not the way they saw life when they were children. Our society's devaluation of marriage makes it easier for people to run at the first sign of trouble. Maybe that's where you are right now.

REWIND

In the space provided, list all of the relationships you have ever had in which there never was a problem.

_____

_____

_____

When you experience an interpersonal problem, what is your initial response?

_____ Ignore it

_____ Overreact to it

_____ Run

_____ Deal with it rationally

_____ Make it a matter of prayer

Life today might not be any different from life a few generations ago, but the challenges are different. Things that people deal with today didn't exist in an agrarian society. When the center of life was the farm, the family pulled together because success in life depended on their teamwork.

Today, however, many marriages look more like a corporate merger. Two independent entities enter into a contractual agreement to pool resources and share living expenses. In exchange, each party receives the benefit of the physical presence of the other (when desired) but also the freedom to pursue personal interests. In the event that the relationship produces offspring, the parties agree to employ the services of a neutral party to see to it that the children have their needs met. In the event that the merger is dissolved, the shared resources shall be maintained by the original owner and custody of the offspring shall be split fifty-fifty. Sounds absurd, doesn't it? But this is the way life is for many families.

JOURNEY THROUGH GOD'S WORD

We know what culture says about divorce, but what does the Bible say? In the Bible, divorce is defined as the breaking of the marriage covenant. It is a dissolution of the pattern of marriage detailed in Genesis 1:27 and 2:21–25.

In Malachi 2:14–16, marriage is described as a covenant between a man and a woman. The marriage relationship was the source for companionship and was the soil in which the knowledge of God was grown. To dissolve that relationship was an affront to God. God hated divorce and warned those who had not yet divorced.

Deuteronomy 24:1–4 details the conditions under which divorce was allowed. According to the Old Testament law, only the man could pursue divorce. The woman could abandon the man, but could not seek divorce. The husband, based on legitimate facts, could issue his wife a certificate of divorce. Once divorced, the woman could remarry, but she could not remarry her original husband. The Old Testament seems to present sexual immorality as the only legitimate grounds for divorce. In the Old Testament, the punishment for adultery was death.

In the New Testament, Jesus said that sexual immorality was the only legitimate reason for divorce. Jesus taught that divorce for any other reason would lead to complications in future marriages. Jesus went so far as to say that God never intended for divorce to occur (Matthew 19:3–12).[2]

The bottom line is that divorce no longer is viewed as it was in biblical times. Because there are no social consequences, people abandon a relationship that could have worked out. Like any other sin, ending the marriage relationship has personal consequences for everyone involved—consequences many people fail to consider in advance.

Divorce has become so common today that we often lose sight of its painful consequences. Even now you may be struggling with feelings of rejection, bitterness, anger, or failure—all of which often follow in the wake of a divorce. Let me assure you that God understands what you are going through, and He still loves you and wants to comfort and guide you. May you find new hope in Christ as you turn to Him, and may God also bring across your path people who can help and encourage you.

BILLY GRAHAM
The Journey

The way you view divorce is connected to your view of family and your understanding of Scripture. The good news is that divorce is not the unpardonable sin. Like lying and greed, divorce can be forgiven and those affected by it restored to a dynamic relationship with God and other people. Maybe life isn't the way you hoped it would be, but no matter where you are, there is a God who loves you and wants the best for your life.

RETHINK

Divorce is . . .

_____ **The norm . . . no one stays married now.**

_____ **A good thing for everyone involved.**

_____ **Not God's perfect plan.**

_____ **Something to look forward to.**

Many couples enter marriage with the idea that their lives will be perfect. Then there is a problem, and they begin to see things the way they really are. Problems escalate; attitudes turn sour, life gets more and more challenging, and the ideas of divorce creep in.

Divorce represents . . .

_____ **An opportunity to get it right the next time.**

_____ **The opportunity to start over with a better mate.**

_____ **A chance to correct a bad decision.**

_____ **A sin against God.**

A minister had the opportunity to perform the renewing of the vows for his parents' fiftieth anniversary. As he was reciting the vows to his mother, the minister got to the part where he said "for better or for worse." He looked up waiting for his mother to repeat the phrase, and she responded by saying "for better . . ." He kept waiting and she quipped, "I'm only interested in better!" The audience laughed. After fifty years of marriage, the couple probably had seen their share of problems and wasn't interested in any more.

It's one thing to have that attitude after fifty years; it's another thing, however, to have that attitude after only a few weeks or months of marriage. The wedding ceremony includes the statement "for as long as we both shall live," not "until one of us decides we're tired of this."

But that doesn't change where you might be. What can you do once your dreams are broken?

REFLECT

Like any other aspect of life, recovering from a perceived failure must be something you do with intentionality. If you have been divorced, there is a process that will lead you to rediscover the joy and peace that accompanies a right relationship with God. The steps to reconciliation can be found in a very familiar story.

The ideal way to reestablish one's relationship with God is pictured in Matthew 7:24–29. This passage is near the end of Jesus' Sermon on the Mount in which He delivered some principles that are foundational to the Christian life.

1. **Pay attention to what God says.**

   The tendency in our culture is to listen to God, the world, and our own desires; mix them all together; and come out with some form of hybrid theology that maximizes God's responsibility to us and minimizes our responsibility to Him. That's not the way it works.

Read Matthew 7:24. What two actions does Jesus require of His hearers?

_____

_____

_____

When Jesus said "these words of mine," He was referencing everything He said in the Sermon on the Mount. The indication is that we can't be selective about what we hear. We are responsible for it all—even the parts we choose to ignore. But hearing the sayings isn't enough. Jesus said that action is required. We must do what He says.

What does this mean to those of us who have let Jesus down with our attitudes and actions? It means we must go back and agree with Jesus. We must confess to Him our rebellion and poor choices and ask for forgiveness. Then and only then will we be firmly established on the rock of God's biblical truth.

2. **Expect the storms.**
   Many people are well prepared for physical storms. We hope the storm will miss us, but we are prepared just in case it hits. We have flashlights, candles, generators, food, batteries, and other things we hope we never have to use.

Read Matthew 7:25. What "storms of life" are you facing right now?

_____

_____

_____

How prepared are you to face the storms of life?

_____

_____

_____

Jesus spoke as if the storms of life are normal. We don't know when they are coming or how they will come, but they are coming. The only way to be strengthened against the storms of life is to establish a strong spiritual foundation.

After seeking forgiveness, the next step is to strengthen our foundations. If not, the next storm of life will have the same effects as the last storm.

What are some things you can do to strengthen your spiritual foundation?

_____

_____

_____

How committed are you to strengthening your spiritual foundation?

_____ It's a nice idea.

_____ I really want this to happen.

_____ I want this but don't know if I'll stick to it.

_____ This is the most important thing I have to do right now.

3. Watch for weaknesses.

The old ways of thinking don't just vanish when you recommit your life to Christ; they tend to become more of a problem. Satan wants you to do anything but grow stronger in your faith. He'll use all sorts of reason-based arguments to challenge your commitment to God.

Read Matthew 7:26–27. What is the ultimate spiritual consequence of not hearing and obeying God's Word?

_____

_____

_____

How do you protect yourself against these problems? Recognize your weaknesses. See those places where Satan can creep in and rob you of your peace and joy. Focus your Bible study so as to strengthen yourself in the areas of your greatest weaknesses.

REACT

The remaining verses of the story reveal what happens when God is lifted up—people are astonished (Matthew 7:28–29). Why? Contrary to the advice given by television talk-show hosts and authors of self-help books, Jesus' advice works every time!

When you face a problem, to whom or what are you most likely to turn?

_____ **A relative**

_____ **Spouse**

_____ **Friend**

_____ **Neighbor**

_____ **Celebrity**

_____ **Self-help book**

_____ **God's Word**

_____ **Pastor or counselor**

How often is the advice of each of the above accurate and relevant to what you are dealing with? (In the space provided, list a percentage).

_____ A relative

_____ Spouse

_____ Friend

_____ Neighbor

_____ Celebrity

_____ Self-help book

_____ God's Word

_____ Pastor or counselor

There was a difference between the teachings of Jesus and the teachings of the scribes. The scribes were the masters of rules; Jesus taught principles. Rules can be applied only in specific situations; principles are universal. Jesus wanted His followers to operate based on His principles. He wants the same for you and me.

What does this mean to us as we face restoration after having let Jesus down? It means we are willing to let Jesus take control of the wheel. If you have been divorced and are considering remarriage, do it God's way this time. If you have failed God in any way, start over His way.

If God discards broken people, there is no one on earth He can use. But through Jesus Christ, God provides a way for us to be renewed and restored. Because of Jesus, you and I have hope!

God understands what you are going through, and He still loves you and wants to comfort and guide you. May you find new hope in Christ and may God bring across you path people to help and encourage you.

BILLY GRAHAM
The Journey

What are three truths you learned in this study, and how will you apply each truth to your daily life?

1. _____

   _____

   _____

   _____

2. _____

_____

_____

_____

3. _____

_____

_____

_____

6

Preventive
Medicine

To GET THE MOST FROM THIS STUDY GUIDE, READ
pages 260–266 of *The Journey*.

---

*God designed marriage and gave it to us. Doesn't it
make sense, therefore, to follow His instructions for
taking care of our marriage? Doesn't it also make sense
to turn to Him when something goes wrong?*

BILLY GRAHAM
The Journey

THINK ABOUT IT

*It is not so important to be serious as it is to be serious about
the important things. The monkey wears an expression
that would do credit to any college student, but the monkey is serious because it itches.*

—ROBERT M. HUTCHINS[1]

*But seek first his kingdom and his righteousness, and all
these things will be given to you as well.*

—MATTHEW 6:33

While sitting in an airport awaiting a flight, you might look out and see a team of people scurrying around the aircraft you are about to board. Some of those people are performing preventive maintenance that is intended to avoid any emergency situations while in flight. It is always reassuring to see those people doing their jobs.

Likewise, we use certain medications to prevent contracting certain illnesses or diseases. We are immunized against diseases that could be life threatening. We take preventive medicine to help us avoid conditions that might make us uncomfortable or unable to function.

If we are going to deal with life's ups and downs, we must be sure to take our spiritual preventive medicine. We must strengthen our immunities so that we can resist things that might otherwise cause us problems. We can't afford to go through life unprepared. Nowhere is this truer than in a marriage.

REWIND

What are some things you routinely do to strengthen your spiritual life?

_____

_____

_____

Based on your response to the question above, how "immunized" against life's dangers are you?

_____ I am already feeling a little weak.

_____ I'm not as strong as I should be.

_____ I'm stronger than I used to be.

_____ I'm prepared—bring it on!

You've probably heard or seen Smokey Bear's slogan, "Only you can prevent forest fires!" It's a saying etched into the minds of Americans with posters, radio, television, and print advertisements. The longest-running public-service campaign ever still runs today. The damage caused by a forest or wildfire takes decades to repair, so prevention was (and is) critical.

The same goes for our marriages. The damage caused by failed marriages is often permanent. In addition to the spouses, there is collateral damage to family members and children. When divorce happens among the members of God's family, the entire family of God is affected. But, just like a forest fire, steps can be taken to prevent it.

JOURNEY THROUGH GOD'S WORD

Throughout the Bible, civilization is identified as existing in one of five structures—open country, village, town, city,

---

and metropolis. In the Old Testament, there is a predominance of the use of village and city. The distinction had little to do with the size of the community. Cities had walls; villages had no walls.

Cities then were much different than they are now. The oldest walled city, Jericho, was approximately ten acres in size. At the height of the Assyrian empire, Nineveh covered more than 1,700 acres or about two and a half square miles. Jerusalem in the time of Solomon covered thirty-three acres and at the time of Jesus less than two hundred acres.

City walls were made from stones or from bricks made from mud. Some walls measured almost three hundred feet thick and over fifty feet tall. The most vulnerable part of the wall was the gate area. The gate was very narrow and had guard towers on either side. The gate, usually made of wood, was braced with metal. Some gates were a series of two or three individual gates. The gates to the city were limited in number so as to minimize the vulnerability of the city. Once inside the gate, a path led from the gate to the city center.[2]

The walled city is a great visual image of the Christian life. The wall protects the Christian from outside threats while the narrow gate limits access to the inside. The path provides access to the very core of a person's being so that anything that comes through the gate can get to the center of a person's life. As a result, we must be careful about what we let through the gate.

Because believers are under attack, they must develop a strong defense system and a strategy for defending themselves. When it comes to marriage, failure to have a defense system in place can be tragic for everyone involved.

RETHINK

What in your view are the three most important parts of a marriage relationship?

_____

_____

_____

_____

Upon what is your list above based?

_____

_____

_____

_____

Engineers can see from minor leaks signs of major flaws in the integrity of a dam. In spite of its benefit, water can be destructive. Over time, small leaks become larger, and eventually the dam can fail.

Marriages can be much the same as a dam. Life's dangers are being held back by the strength of the relationship. Small things begin to get through the barrier, and soon the small things are big things and the problems are immense. The structure of the relationship begins to give way and eventually crashes, leaving the surrounding area devastated.

Many marriages that end in divorce could be salvaged if the husband and wife invested time in making the marriage stronger. Preventive maintenance in marriage is the key to success.

What are some things you can do to strengthen your marriage and/or other significant relationships?

_____

_____

_____

_____

Are you doing these things? Why or why not?

_____

_____

_____

_____

REFLECT

Anything worth having is worth working for. Certainly in today's world, a healthy marriage is something to be desired. But how do we get one? Let's look at three steps for keeping the flame alive.

1. **Commit your marriage relationship to God.**

   The only One who can fix a marriage is the One who made it—God. Marriage was God's idea. We have violated His patent and made it into something that was never intended. A good marriage is not a 50-50 arrangement; it is a 100-100 arrangement. Each marriage partner must give 100 percent if the marriage relationship is going to work. In addition, each spouse must give 100 percent to God.

What does it mean to commit your marriage to God?

_____ To have the ceremony performed by a minister

_____ To have the ceremony performed in a church

_____ To have someone pray at the ceremony

_____ To give each day of marriage to God as an offering to Him

Committing your marriage to God means taking your vows seriously. When you made your vows, you made them to each other and to God. Your vows require faithfulness. Faithfulness is the opposite of adultery. You can't be faithful and commit adultery.

Read Exodus 20:14. What does this commandment say?

_____

_____

_____

Read Proverbs 6:32. What is the ultimate danger of adultery?

_____

_____

_____

What are you going to do when the opportunity to commit adultery comes along?

_____

_____

_____

Committing your marriage to God also means growing together in your relationship with Christ. In addition to growing spiritually on our own, we are commanded to grow together spiritually.

Which of the following is or will become an important part of your marriage relationship?

_____ Praying together

_____ Reading God's Word together

_____ Going to church together

_____ Having fellowship together with other Christians

If you aren't doing these things, why aren't you? If you are, what is happening to your marriage relationship as a result of your spiritual togetherness?

_____

_____

_____

_____

Read 1 Thessalonians 5:11. What is our responsibility to each other?

_____

_____

_____

2. **Commit yourself to your marriage.**

   It is easy to get distracted with work and hobbies and everything else. Unless we are intentional about it, our marriages can take a backseat to everything else we are doing.

Read Ephesians 5:25. Reread this verse substituting the husband's name for _husbands_. What is the instruction of this verse?

_____

_____

_____

Committing your marriage to God means giving it priority. It is your most important earthly relationship, so you must make it a priority.

What are some things you do on a regular basis? What is the impact of each on your marriage? Place an X on the line for each item listed.

	None	Significant
Travel	---	
Hobbies	---	
Socialize	---	
Work	---	
Read	---	
Exercise	---	
Sleep	---	
Other	---	

Your marriage is of major importance to God. How important is it to you?

3. **Treat each other with affection and respect.**
   People will seek affection and respect somewhere. For a married couple, the ideal place is inside the

relationship. However, when we become so self-centered that we don't offer affection and respect, we are opening the city gate to let in the enemy.

Read Ephesians 5:33. What is the instruction in this passage?

_____

_____

_____

_____

Read 1 Peter 3:7. How are husbands to treat their wives?

_____

_____

_____

_____

One of the best ways to show your respect for each other is to learn to communicate. Communication has two parts—talking and listening.

How would you describe your communication with your spouse?

_____ Mindless chatter

_____ Informational

_____ One-way

_____ Real communication in which we listen and talk

Don't let a day go by without telling your spouse that you love them. Show your affection spontaneously and frequently. A hug, a kiss, a gentle pat or squeeze of the arm, even a glance at each other can say, "I still love you." In addition, be courteous, tender, and thoughtful to each other. It always saddens me to hear a husband put down his wife with sarcasm or a cutting remark, or a wife correct her husband or scold him like a little boy, especially in front of others. Be an encourager; learn to forgive each other as well.

BILLY GRAHAM
The Journey

Learn to express your love for your spouse—unexpected expressions of love often are the most meaningful. Go on dates, buy flowers, and send cards for no special reason other than express-ing your love. Be willing to compromise your wants for the sake of your spouse. Go to a sporting event even though you don't like the sport; take your wife shopping and be patient while she tries on everything in the store and buys nothing. Learn to give as well as take in the relationship.

Learn to laugh together. Life is too short to take so seriously. Laughter really is good medicine. Don't laugh at your spouse; laugh with him or her.

Read Hebrews 3:13. How can you encourage your spouse daily?

_____

_____

_____

Take away the burdens your spouse is carrying. We need the help of each other to make it through this life. In Galatians 6:2, Paul told the Galatians that it is necessary that we carry each other's burdens. By listening and investing time with your spouse, you can lift the burden and be a picture of God in action.

What if you are unmarried? God calls some people to remain single. In being single, they have opportunities to serve God in ways many married people can't. Don't look at marriage as being more important than serving God. Serve Him first and, if He leads you to marry, marry the right person at the right time. Until then, keep yourself pure.

Read 1 Timothy 5:22. In what ways are you protecting your purity?

_____

_____

_____

_____

REACT

In His infinite wisdom, God gave us a design through which we are made better. When we marry within God's plan for us, our lives are enriched and our ministries extended.

We should never take our marriages, spouses, or families for granted. God has uniquely put us together for a purpose. We can do more together than we ever could do apart.

Write a note of commitment to your present or future spouse. Express in your own words the truths that this lesson has highlighted. When the time is right, put these words into a card

and mail it to your spouse. If you aren't married, keep it as a reminder of your commitment to purity.

> *One of the ways we demonstrate our love for God is by demonstrating our love for our spouses. Christ sacrificed Himself out of love for His people, and a husband should make sacrifices out of love for his wife.*
>
> BILLY GRAHAM
> *The Journey*

Read 1 Peter 3:3–4. What is more important—inner beauty or outward appearance?

Does your life reflect this truth? Why or why not?

_____

_____

_____

What are three truths you learned in this study, and how will you apply each truth to your daily life?

1. _____

_____

_____

2. _____

_____

_____

3. _____

_____

_____

_____

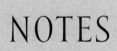

NOTES

CHAPTER 1

1. Bob Kelly, *Worth Repeating*, 2003. Grand Rapids, MI: Kregel Publications, 82.
2. *Holman Illustrated Bible Dictionary*, 2005. Nashville, TN: B&H, 1685–1686.

CHAPTER 2

1. Bob Kelly, *Worth Repeating*, 82.

CHAPTER 3

1. Bob Kelly, *Worth Repeating*, 223.
2. *Holman Illustrated Bible Dictionary*, 1082–1083.

CHAPTER 4

1. Bob Kelly, *Worth Repeating*, 171.
2. *Holman Illustrated Bible Dictionary*, 282.

CHAPTER 5

1. Bob Kelly, *Worth Repeating*, 110.
2. *Holman Illustrated Bible Dictionary*, 435.

CHAPTER 6

1. Bob Kelly, *Worth Repeating*, 283.
2. *Holman Illustrated Bible Dictionary*, 301–302.

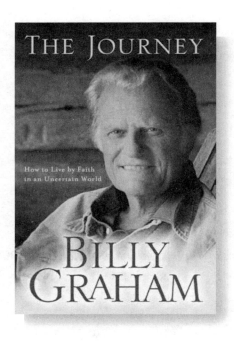

Billy Graham is respected and loved around the world. *The Journey* is his magnum opus, the culmination of a lifetime of experience and ministry. With insight that comes only from a life spent with God, this book is filled with wisdom, encouragement, hope, and inspiration for anyone who wants to live a happier, more fulfilling life.

978-0-8499-1887-2 (PB)